LIFE CYCLES

Apple Trees

by Robin Nelson

first step nonfiction

D1059067

Lerner Publications Company · Minneapolis

This is an apple tree.

There are many kinds of apples.

How do apple trees grow?

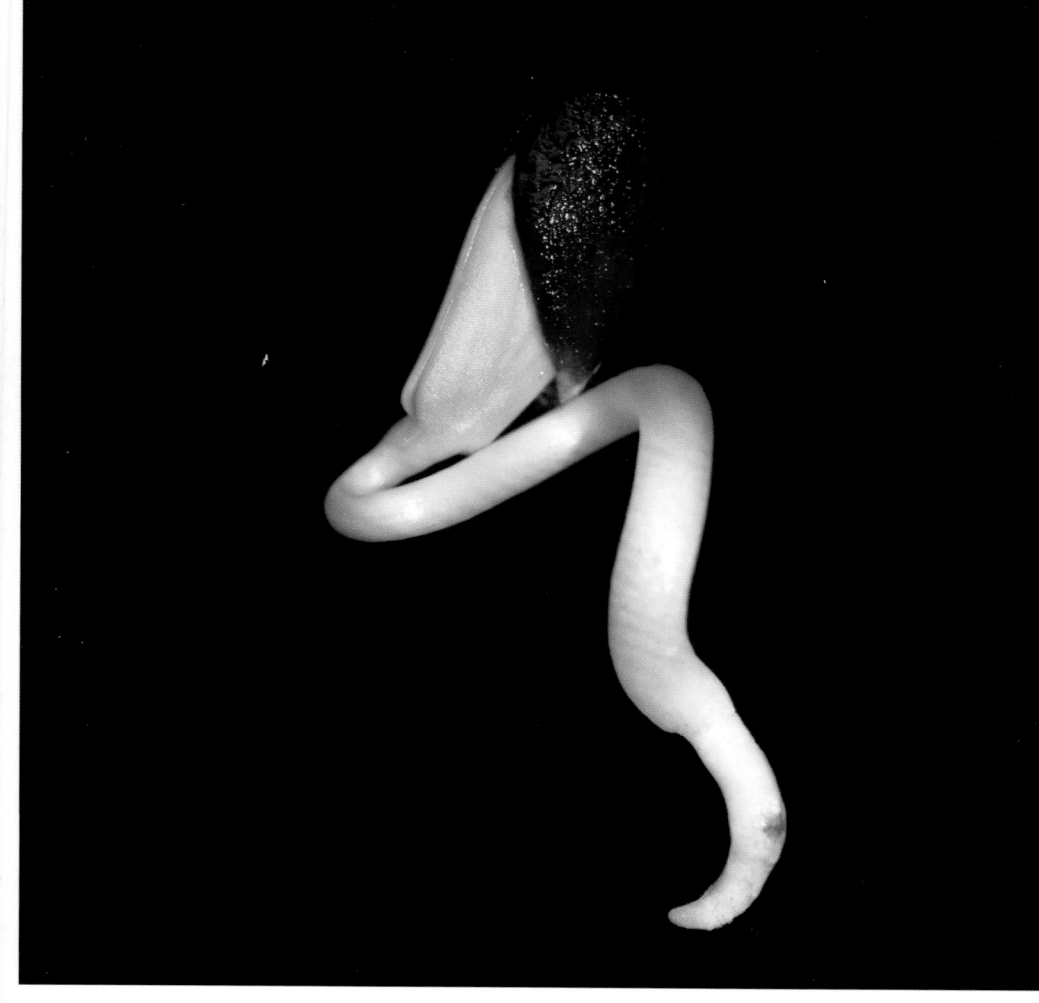

First, an apple seed grows
roots.

Next, a **shoot** grows out of the ground.

The young tree grows leaves
and gets taller.

It is called a **sapling**.

After a few years, it is a tree.

One year, flower **buds** appear.

The buds open, and the
tree is covered with flowers.

Bees visit the flowers.

The flowers fall off, and tiny green apples begin to grow.

The apples grow big
and red.

In the fall, apples are ready
to be picked.

Some apples fall or are carried away.

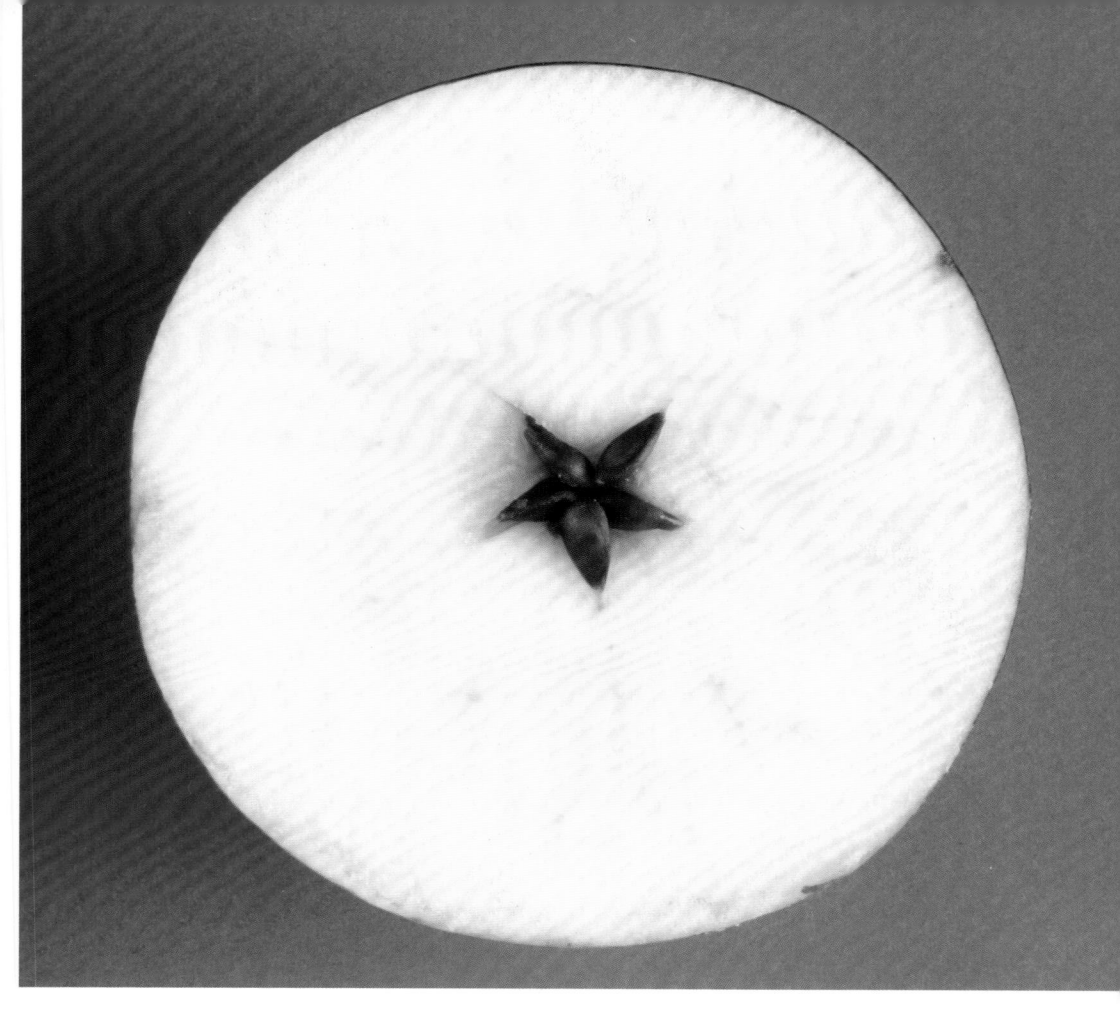

The seeds inside the apples
could grow into new trees.

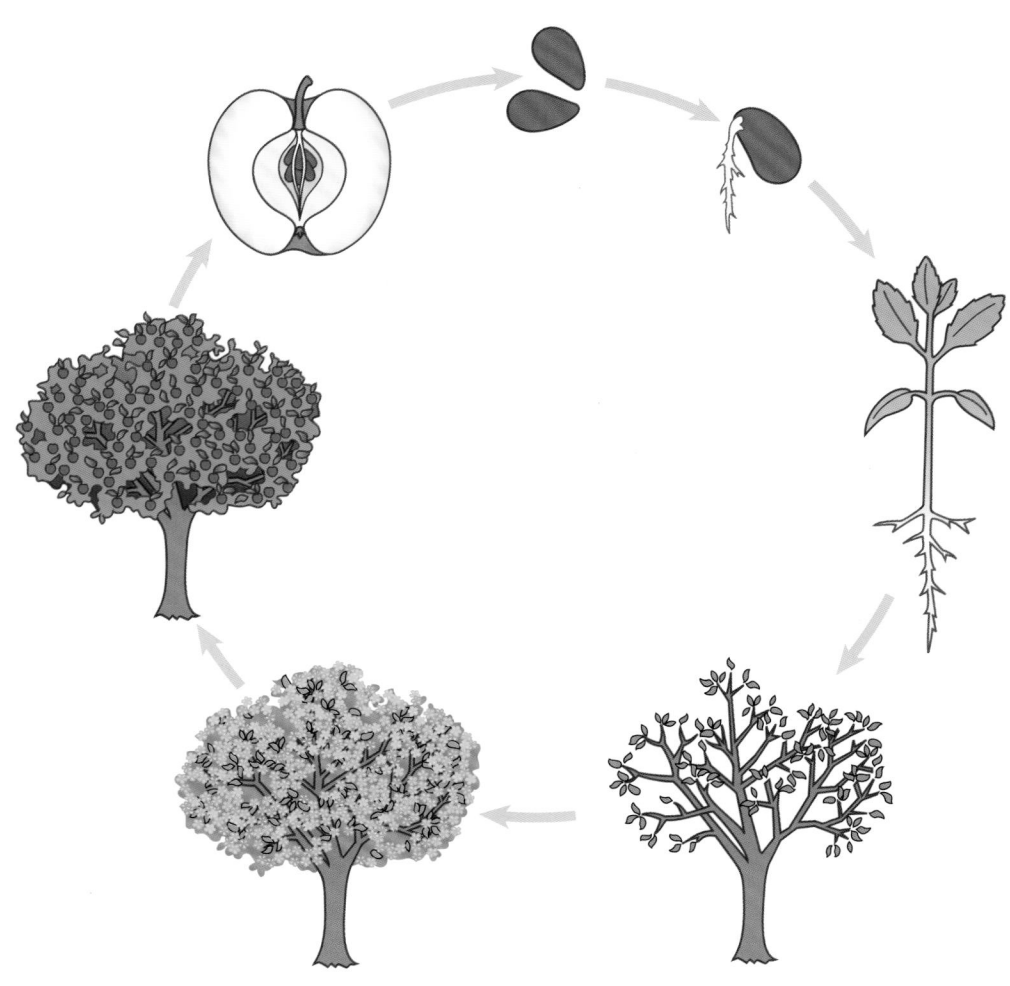

18

Apple Trees

Apples come in many sizes and colors. Apples are grown all over the world. China grows the most apples of any country in the world.

It takes five to seven years for an apple seed to grow into a tree and grow its first apples. From then on, it grows apples every year.

Apple Tree Facts

 Most apples are eaten just as they are. You can also make apple cider, apple butter, apple pie, applesauce, and many other things!

 Johnny Appleseed was a man who traveled across America planting apple trees.

 Some apple trees are very small and could fit in your bedroom. Others can grow to be 40 feet tall.

 Apple farmers do not grow apple trees from seeds. They cut part of a grown apple tree and attach it to another tree stem. This grows into an apple tree.

 October is National Apple Month. Most apples are picked in October.

 Most apples are picked by hand in the fall.

Glossary

 **buds** – a flower that has not opened yet

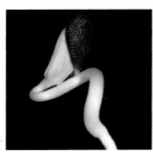 **roots** – parts of a plant that grow down into the ground

 **sapling** – a young tree

 **shoot** – a plant that has just started to grow

Index

The photographs in this book are reproduced through the courtesy of: © Karlene Schwartz, pp. 2, 10, 13, 22 (top); © Julie Caruso/Independent Picture Service, p. 3; © Marta Johnson, p. 4; © Scott Camazine /Alamy, pp. 5, 22 (second from top); © Dwight Kuhn , pp. 6, 12, 22 (bottom); © Nigel Cattlin/Visuals Unlimited, Inc., p. 7; © Johner Images/Getty Images, pp. 8, 22 (second from bottom); © Bronwyn Photo-Fotolia.com , p. 9; © audaxl-Fotolia.com , p. 11; ©Mitch Wojnarowicz / Amsterdam Recorder / The Image Works , p. 15; © SuperND-Fotolia.com , p. 16, © Todd Strand/ Independent Picture Service, p. 17. Illustrations by © Laura Westlund/Independent Picture Service.

Front Cover: © iStockphoto.com/Brian McEntire.

Lerner Publications Company
A division of Lerner Publishing Group, Inc.
241 First Avenue North
Minneapolis, MN 55401 U.S.A.

Website address: www.lernerbooks.com

Library of Congress Cataloging-in-Publication Data

Nelson, Robin, 1971–
    Apple trees / by Robin Nelson.
        p.   cm. — (First step nonfiction. Plant life cycles)
    Includes index.
    ISBN: 978–0–7613–4071–3 (lib. bdg. : alk. paper)
    ISBN: 978–0–7613–5162–7 (eBook)
    1. Apples—Life cycles—Juvenile literature. I. Title. II. Series.
SB363.N45 2009
    634'.11—dc22   2008033734

Manufactured in the United States of America
3 – PC – 8/1/13